Also by John Updike

POEMS

The Carpentered Hen (1958) · *Telephone Poles* (1963) · *Midpoint* (1969) · *Tossing and Turning* (1977) · *Facing Nature* (1985) · *Collected Poems 1953–1993* (1993) · *Americana* (2001)

NOVELS

The Poorhouse Fair (1959) · *Rabbit, Run* (1960) · *The Centaur* (1963) · *Of the Farm* (1965) · *Couples* (1968) · *Rabbit Redux* (1971) · *A Month of Sundays* (1975) · *Marry Me* (1976) · *The Coup* (1978) · *Rabbit Is Rich* (1981) · *The Witches of Eastwick* (1984) · *Roger's Version* (1986) · *S.* (1988) · *Rabbit at Rest* (1990) · *Memories of the Ford Administration* (1992) · *Brazil* (1994) · *Rabbit Angstrom* (1995) · *In the Beauty of the Lilies* (1996) · *Toward the End of Time* (1997) · *Gertrude and Claudius* (2000) · *Seek My Face* (2002) · *Villages* (2004) · *Terrorist* (2006) · *The Widows of Eastwick* (2008)

SHORT STORIES

The Same Door (1959) · *Pigeon Feathers* (1962) · *Olinger Stories* (a selection, 1964) · *The Music School* (1966) · *Bech: A Book* (1970) · *Museums and Women* (1972) · *Problems and Other Stories* (1979) · *Too Far to Go* (a selection, 1979) · *Bech Is Back* (1982) · *Trust Me* (1987) · *The Afterlife* (1994) · *Bech at Bay* (1998) · *Licks of Love* (2000) · *The Complete Henry Bech* (2001) · *The Early Stories: 1953–1975* (2003) · *My Father's Tears and Other Stories* (2009) · *The Maples Stories* (2009)

ESSAYS AND CRITICISM

Assorted Prose (1965) · *Picked-Up Pieces* (1975) · *Hugging the Shore* (1983) · *Just Looking* (1989) · *Odd Jobs* (1991) · *Golf Dreams: Writings on Golf* (1996) · *More Matter* (1999) · *Still Looking* (2005) · *Due Considerations* (2007)

PLAY

Buchanan Dying (1974)

MEMOIRS

Self-Consciousness (1989)

CHILDREN'S BOOKS

The Magic Flute (1962) · *The Ring* (1964) · *A Child's Calendar* (1965) · *Bottom's Dream* (1969) · *A Helpful Alphabet of Friendly Objects* (1996)

ENDPOINT

John Updike

ENDPOINT

and Other Poems

Alfred A. Knopf · New York

2009

THIS IS A BORZOI BOOK
PUBLISHED BY ALFRED A. KNOPF

www.aaknopf.com

ISBN: 978-0-307-27286-7
LCCN: 2009922927

Manufactured in the United States of America
First Edition

ACKNOWLEDGMENTS

Some of these poems were previously published in *American Poetry Review*, *American Scholar*, *Atlantic Monthly*, *Boston Review*, *Light*, *Literary Imagination*, *Lord John Press*, *New York Times Book Review*, *Ontario Review*, *Oxford Review*, *Poetry*, *Reading* (Pennsylvania) *Eagle*, and *Van Gogh's Ear*. The following first appeared in *The New Yorker*: "Country Music"; "Duet on Mars"; "Evening Concert, Sainte-Chapelle"; "March Birthday 2002"; "Saguaros"; "Stolen"; and "To a Well-Connected Mouse." The poems "Frankie Laine," "Lucian Freud," and "Wee Irish Suite" first appeared in *The New York Review of Books*.

CONTENTS

For MARTHA, who asked for one more book:
here it is, with all my love

C

Sonnets

CONTENTS

For Martha, who asked for one more book:
here it is, with all my love

Light and Personal

Endpoint

ENDPOINT

March Birthday 2002, and After

Beverly Farms, MA

Mild winter, then a birthday burst of snow.
A faint neuralgia, flitting tooth-root to
knee and shoulder-joint, a vacant head,
too many friendly wishes to parry,
too many cakes. Oh, let the years alone!
They pile up if we manage not to die,
glass dollars in the bank, dry pages on
the shelf. The boy I was no longer smiles

a greeting from the bottom of the well,
blue sky behind him from a story book.
The Philco sings out “Hi-yo” by his sickbed;
he thinks that Mother, Father, mailman, and
the wheezy doctor with his wide black bag
exist for him, and so they do, or did.

*

Wife absent for a day or two, I wake
alone and older, the storm that aged me
distilled to a skin of reminiscent snow,
so thin a blanket blades of grass show through.
Snow makes white shadows, there behind the yews,
dissolving in the sun’s slant kiss, and pools
itself across the lawn as if to say,
Give me another hour, then I’ll go.

The lawn's begun to green. Beyond the Bay—
where I have watched, these twenty years, dim ships
ply the horizon, feeding oil to Boston,
and blinking lights descend, night after night,
to land unseen at Logan—low land implies
a sprawl of other lives, beneath torn clouds.

*

Raw days, though spring has been declared.
I settle in, to that decade in which,
I'm told, most people die. Then, flying south,
I wonder why houses in their patterned crowds
look white, whatever their earthbound colors,
from the air. Golf courses, nameless rivers.
The naked Connecticut woods hold veins
of madder like the green veins of the sea.

The pilot takes us down Manhattan's spine—
the projects, Riverside cathedral, Midtown
bristling up like some coarse porcupine.
We seem too low, my palms begin to sweat.
The worst can happen, we know it from the news.
Age I must, but die I would rather not.

*

Not yet. Home safe. New England's vernal drought
has taken a hit this week of sleety rain.
Spent harbingers, the snowdrops lie
in drenched, bedraggled clumps, their tired news
becoming weeds. The crocuses drink in
the leaden air and spread their stained-glass cups
to catch the filtered sun clapboards reflect,
and daffodils grow leggy like young girls.

Nature is never bored, and we whose lives
are linearly pinned to these aloof,
self-fascinated cycles can't complain,
though aches and pains and even dreams a-crawl
with wood lice of decay give pause to praise.
Birthday, death day—what day is not both?

03/18/03

Beverly Farms

Birthday begun in fog, shot through with light—
"eating the snow," they used to say. The *Globe*
this morning adds a name to those I share
the date with: Wilson Pickett, Brad Dourif,
F. W. de Klerk, Vanessa Williams,
my pal George Plimpton, plus Hawaiian statehood.
The name is Queen Latifah, whom I've seen
in several recent movie hits. Sweet smile.

A day so blank, I take a walk, the way
my parents used to do in Sunday's calm.
Through woods, in boots, the snowmelt turning leaves
to soggy mats. A lack of tracks: I am
the first to walk this path this snowbound spring,
an Adam being nibbled like old ice.

*

The winds of war, warm winds in desert dust,
have been unleashed, the fifth war of my life,
not counting the Cold one, and skirmishes.

Protestors dust off Vietnam's gaudy gear
and mount their irreproachable high nags
called Peace, Diplomacy, and Love.
I think that love fuels war like gasoline,
and crying peace curdles the ears of doves.

Yet something is awry, no doubt of it.
Out on the Bay, a strange steel spider crawls
among our islands, glaring bright at night.
Time was when this white house, with its broad view,
wore blackout shades and watched the iron sea
for submarines. A child then now is old.

*

My parents seemed to sail ahead of me
like ships receding to destinations where
I'd be forgotten. "Wait up!" I wailed,
those Sunday walks a faint pretaste of death.
Today, I tread with care the icy path
and climb the beachside boulders well aware
of how a slip, a misjudged step, might crack
my skull and there I'd lie like limp sea-wrack.

The well-lit thing at night, a neighbor claims,
is laying pipe, for natural gas, to Salem.
But under water? It carries a crane
and freezing men we cannot see—poor men,
who serve from bleak necessity campaigns
conceived in cozy offices. Wait up!

Tucson Birthday, 2004

Ocotillo leafs out beside the porch rail—
saw-teeth of green assault the sky's nude blue.
The cactus wrens chirp in the cholla's shade.
Beyond, the tennis players call it quits.
Downtown, miles stretch like melting tar
beneath the car wheels; desert distances
suffuse the asphalt of the many malls
with fuming, SUV-infested haste.

My mother dreamed of Tucson once, when I
was a boy with no desire to move
or leave my father, which was part of the deal.
Now here I am, the very day she bore me.
I thought my birthday, here, would prove unreal,
but time and sun are not so smoothly fooled.

*

Sun damage—the skin does not forget:
Crane Beach, the Caribbean, hoeing shirtless
the Pennsylvania bean-rows. Cells remember
and wrinkle, pucker, draw up in a knot
the doctor's liquid nitrogen attacks.
And yet, the illusion lingers, light is good
as sent down by the sun, that nearby star
that flattens like a fist, and burns to kill.

They come, the retirees, to bake away
their juicy lifetime jobs, their fertile prime's
no longer potent jism. And I, I scratch
this inconclusive ode to age. It feels

immortal, the sun's dark kiss. The prickly pear
has ears like Mickey Mouse, my first love.

*

To copy comic strips, stretched prone
upon the musty carpet—Mickey's ears,
the curl in Donald's bill, the bulbous nose
of Barney Google, Captain Easy's squint—
what bliss! The paper creatures loved me back
by going about their businesses each day,
and in the corner of my eye, my blind
grandfather's black shoes jiggled when he sang.

The West, our better half, has turned obese.
Vast movie houses hold a quiet handful
of senior citizens bemused by shows
of closely shaved, inane obscenity.
At city limits, numb saguaros hail
with lifted arms the guzzling sunset rush.

The Author Observes His Birthday, 2005

A life poured into words—apparent waste
intended to preserve the thing consumed.
For who, in that unthinkable future
when I am dead, will read? The printed page
was just a half-millennium's brief wonder,
Erasmus's and Luther's Gutenberg-
perfected means of propagating truth,
or lies, screw-pressed one folio at a time.

A world long dulled by plagues and plainsong warmed
to metal's kiss, the cunning kerns and serifs,
the Gothic spears and rounded Roman forms,
the creamy margins smartly justified,
the woodcuts showing naked Mother Eve:
a rage to read possessed the peasantry.

*

The church was right; the Bible freed
spelled trouble. Literate Protestants waged war,
and smashed the Lady Chapels all to Hell,
new-style. No Pope, no priests, no Purgatory—
instead, clear windows and the pilgrim soul,
that self which tribal ways suppressed, and whose
articulation asked a world of books.

A small-town Lutheran tot, I fell in love
with comic strips, Benday, and talk balloons.
The daily paper brought us headlined war
and labor strife; I passed them by en route
to the funnies section, where no one died
or even, saving Chic Young's *Blondie*, aged.

*

My harried father told me, "Dog eat dog."
I opted for a bloodless universe
of inked imaginings. My mother's books
from college—Shakespeare and Sir Walter Scott,
Lane Cooper, Sinclair Lewis, H. G. Wells—
made peaceful patterns with their faded spines.
I didn't open them, unleashing dogs
too real for me, but sniffed their gentle smell

of paper, glue, and cloth. My many dreams
of future puissance—as a baseball star,
test pilot, private eye, cartoonist, or
as Errol Flynn or Fred Astaire—did not
include a hope to be the hidden hand
and mind behind some musty, clothbound maze.

*

But, then, to see my halt words strut in type!
To see *The Poorhouse Fair* in galley proofs
and taste the candy jacket Harry Ford
cooked up for me! And then to have my spines
line up upon the shelf, one more each year,
however out of kilter ran my life!
I drank up women's tears and spat them out
as 10-point Janson, Roman and *ital.*

When Blanche and Alfred took me out to lunch
he sent the wine right back. *How swell,* I thought.
Bill Maxwell's treat was Japanese; we sat
cross-legged on the floor and ate fish raw,
like gulls. In suit and tie, an author proved
to be, like "fuck" in print, respectable.

*

Back then, my children, in those simpler years
before all firms were owned by other firms,
the checks would come imprinted with a dog,
a bounding Borzoi, or the profile of
a snooty figment, Eustace Tilley. He
was like a god to me, the guardian
of excellence; he weighed my mailed-in words
and paid a grand or so for tales he liked.

A thousand dollars then meant we could eat
for months. A poem might buy a pair of shoes.
My life, my life with children, was a sluice
that channeled running water to my pan;
by tilting it, and swirling lightly, I
at end of day might find a fleck of gold.

*

A writer, stony-hearted as he seems,
needs nurturing. My mother's Remington
tip-tapped through all my childhood fevers, aimed
at realms beyond the sickbed, porch, and yard.
Though Pennsylvania Dutch, she fell in love
with Spain, its wistful knights and Catholic queens
and tried, *tip-tap*, to stretch her Remington
across the gap of space and time, and failed.

I took off from her failure. Katharine White
saw in me fodder for her magazine,
and Judith Jones, from 1960 on,
abetted all my books, an editor
excelling as encourager, who found
the good intention even in a botch.

*

My aspirations met indulgent spirits
long resident in Ink, Inc.'s castle keep:
I somehow wasn't Jewish, which made me
minority and something of a pet.
When Mr. Shawn, the magus in his cave,
went pink, he whispered friendly oracles.
Urbane and dapper Sidney Jacobs, head
of Knopf production, gave a pica stick

to me that I still measure by, and books
of fonts I still consult. Wry Howard Moss
allowed my poems safe passage now and then.
A host of minions supervised my grammar;
a brace of wives forgave my doubtful taste.

*

Today, the author hits three score thirteen,
an age his father, woken in the night
by pressure on his heart, fell short of. Still,
I scribble on. My right hand occupies
the center of my vision, faithful old
five-fingered beast of burden, dappled with
some psoriatic spots I used to hate,
replaced by spots of damage the crude sun-cure

extracted from my dermis through the years.
The beast is dry and mottled, shedding skin
as minutes drop from life, a wristy piece
of dogged ugliness, its labors meant
to carve from language beauty, that beauty which
lifts free of flesh to find itself in print.

My Mother at Her Desk

My mother knew non-publication's shame,
obscurity's abyss, where blind hands flog
typewriter keys in hopes of raising up
the magic combination that will sell.
Instead, brown envelopes return, bent double

in letter slots to flop on the foyer floor,
or else abandoned flat within the tin
of the rural mailbox, as insects whirr.

She studied How To, diagrammed Great Plots
some correspondence course assigned, read Mann,
Flaubert, and Faulkner, looking for the clue,
the "open sesame" to fling the cave door back
and flood with light the shadows in her heart
to turn them golden, worth their weight in cash.

*

Mine was to be the magic gift instead,
propelled to confidence by mother-love
and polished for the New York market by
New England's wintry flair for education.
But hers was the purer ambition, hatched
of country childhood in the silences
of crops accruing, her sole companions birds
whose songs and names she taught herself to know.

Her gray head cocked, she'd say, "The chickadee
feels lonely!" Bent above a book, she'd lift
her still-young face and say, "Such ugly words!"
as if each stood alone. *No, no,* I thought,
context is all. But I was male, and made
to make a mark, while Mother typed birdsong.

Dry Spell, 2006

In Arizona's drought, even cacti
die; the prickly pears are pancake-flat
with no more rain to plump them up, and blanch
to lavender instead of green. Iraq
continues like a curtainless bad play,
the Tucson *Star* headlines the daily bust,
and Barry Bonds limps close to Babe Ruth's record.
Amid all this, I age another notch.

Dear Lord, have I become too poor a thing
to save? My pencil creeps across this page
unsure where next to go. My children phone
from far-off islands, all their lives in flux
while mine has petrified, a desert rock
to take their superstitious bearings by.

*

Today my mate of thirty years and I
explored the grid that fills our foothills view
and bought two oleander plants to screen
our porch from passing cars, or them from us.
How touchingly we scrambled on the rocks,
our footing poor, to pour out Miracle-Gro
(the blue of Listerine) on wilting plants
that mutely guard our island in the sun.

She gave me, at my own discreet request,
a dictionary full of words I keep
forgetting, and a watch whose battery
is guaranteed to last ten years, at least.

Ten years! It will tick in my coffin while
my bones continue to deteriorate.

*

Our view—in other seasons, of the North
Atlantic, luminous and level, fringed
by greenery that goes, all imperceptibly,
from bud to leaf to blaze to cold, bare twig—
at night resembles, in its lateral sweep,
the other one, two thousand miles away.
The city, in its valley lying flat
as golden water, twinkles, ripples, breathes,

streetlights deflected downward to avoid
bleaching the sky for the observatories
whose giant-geared and many-mirrored eyes
peer upward from some local mountaintops.
These mountains hang to the south like blue clouds
that would, back East, past Hull and Hingham, bring rain.

Birthday Shopping, 2007

Today, in Tucson, Mrs. U. and I
drove through the downtown grid, where cowboys in
white pickup trucks turn left against the light,
to Best Buy's big box, to buy a back-up laptop.
Brave world! The geeks in matching shirts
talked gigabytes to girls with blue tattoos
and nostril studs, and guys with ropey arms
packed pixel-rich home-entertainment screens.
Hi-def is in. Attempting to prepare

our obsolescing heads for crashing waves
of new technology, we cruised an aisle
of duplicated, twitching imagery
and came upon, as if upon an elf
asleep on forest moss, a Chinese child.

*

It was a girl, aged two or three, in bangs
and plastic bow and tiny shiny dress
and round-toed Velcroed shoes, supine
upon a cardboard carton, inches from
a coruscating hi-def plasma screen,
her face as close and rapt as at an udder,
motionlessly drinking something in,
an underwater scene of garish fish.

An older sister gazed her fill nearby;
at last we spotted their adoptive ma
haggling fine points several clerks away.
Exquisite in her peace, the alien child
had found a parent, bright and slightly warm,
while I, a birthday boy, was feeling lost.

*

In Pomeroy's Department Store, I lost
my mother's hand three score and more than ten
long years ago. So panicky I wet
my pants a drop or two, I felt space widen;
when someone not my mother took my hand,
I burbled, unable to cough up who
I was, so unforeseeably alone
amid these aisles of goods, so unlike home.

Not so this transfixed little pixie here
among the pixels, stiller than if asleep.
Electromagnetism holds her fast,
secure within the infotainment web,
that sticky and spontaneous conflux
of self-advertisement and spam and porn.

*

Well, even Roosevelt's sunk Depression world—
Atlantis at the bottom of a life,
descried through sliding thicknesses of time—
had radio and cinema to love,
and love we did, in haste to make the new
our own, to wield against our elders, dull
with all the useless stuff they'd had to learn
when they were helpless children just like us.

Signals beyond their ken transported us—
Jack Benny's stately pauses, Errol Flynn's
half-smile, the songs we learned to smoke to, ads
in magazines called slicks, the comic strips,
realer than real, a Paradise that if
we held our breaths, we could ascend to, free.

*

In the beginning, Culture does beguile us,
but Nature gets us in the end. My skin,
I notice now that I am seventy-five,
hangs loose in ripples like those dunes on Mars
that tell us life may have existed there—
monocellular slime in stagnant pools.
After a Tucson movie, some man in
the men's room mirror lunged toward me

with wild small eyes, white hair, and wattled neck—
who could he be, so hostile and so weird,
so due for disposal, like a popcorn bag
vile with its inner film of stale, used grease?
Where was the freckled boy who used to peek
into the front-hall mirror, off to school?

*

Its cracked brown frame and coat of mercury
going thin behind the glass embodied time,
as did the fraying rugs, the kitchen chairs,
the four adults that shared the house with me.
In Pennsylvania then, the past had settled in
to be the present. Nothing greatly changed:
milk came to the porch, and mail through the slot,
coal down the loud chute, and ice in crazed cakes

on the iceman's leathern back. My grandparents
moved through the rooms in a fog of dailiness,
younger then than I am now, and my parents,
not forty—can it be?—expressed their youth
by quarreling and slamming doors. Our old
clock ticked, and dust, God's pixels, calmly danced.

Spirit of '76

Cypresses have one direction, up,
but sometimes desert zephyrs tousle one
so that a branch or two will stick straight out—
a hatchling fallen from the nest,

a broken leg a limp will not forget,
a lock of cowlicked hair that spurns the comb.
Aspiring like steeples inky green,
they spear the sun-bleached view with nodding tips.

How not to think of death? Its ghastly blank
lies underneath your dreams, that once gave rise
to horn-hard, conscienceless erections.
Just so, your waking brain no longer stiffens
with careless inspirations—urgent news
spilled in clenched spasms on the virgin sheets.

*

Here in this place of arid clarity,
two thousand miles from where my souvenirs
collect a cozy dust, the piled produce
of bald ambition pulling ignorance,
I see clear through to the ultimate page,
the silence I dared break for my small time.
No piece was easy, but each fell finished,
in its shroud of print, into a book-shaped hole.

Be with me, words, a little longer; you
have given me my quitclaim in the sun,
sealed shut my adolescent wounds, made light
of grownup troubles, turned to my advantage
what in most lives would be pure deficit,
and formed, of those I loved, more solid ghosts.

*

Our annual birthday do: dinner at
the Arizona Inn for only two.
White tablecloth, much cutlery, décor

in somber dark-beamed territorial style.
No wine, thank you. Determined to prolong
our second marriages, we gave that up,
with cigarettes. We toast each other's health
in water and a haze of candlelight.

My imitation of a proper man,
white-haired and wed to aging loveliness,
has fit me like a store-bought suit, not quite
my skin, but wearing well enough until,
at ceremony's end, my wife points out
I don't know how to use a finger bowl.

A Lightened Life

Beverly Farms, 4/14/08

A lightened life: last novel proofs FedExed—
the final go-through, back-and-forthing till
all adjectives seemed wrong, inferior to
an almost-glimpsed unreal alternative
spoken perhaps on Mars—and taxes, state
and federal, mailed. They were much more this year,
thanks to the last novel's mild success,
wry fruit of terror-fear and author's tours.

Checks mailed, I stopped for gas, and plumb forgot
how to release the gas-cap door. True,
I'd been driving a rented car for weeks. But, too,
this morning I couldn't do the computer code

for the *accent grave* in *fin-de-siècle*, one
of my favorite words. What's up? What's left of me?

Euonymus 11/02/08

My window tells me the euonymus
arrives now at the last and deepest shade
of red, before its leaves let go. One of
my grandsons leaves a phone message for me;
his voice has deepened. A cold that wouldn't let go
is now a cloud upon my chest X-ray:
pneumonia. My house is now a cage
I prowl, window to window, as I wait

for time to take away the cloud within.
The rusty autumn gold is glorious.
Blue jays and a small gray bird, white-chested,
decline to join the seasonal escape
and flit on bushes below. Is this an end?
I hang, half-healthy, here, and wait to see.

Oblong Ghosts 11/6/08

A wake-up call? It seems that death has found
the portals it will enter by: my lungs,
pathetic oblong ghosts, one paler than
the other on the doctor's viewing screen.

Looking up "pneumonia," I learn
it can, like an erratic dog, turn mean
and snap life short for someone under two
or "very old (over 75)."

Meanwhile, our President Obama waits
downstairs to be unwrapped and I, a child
transposed toward Christmas Day in Shillington—
air soft and bright, a touch of snow outside—
pause here, one hand upon the banister,
and breathe the scent of fresh-cut evergreens.

Hospital 11/23–27/08

Mass. General, Boston

Benign big blond machine beyond all price,
it swallows us up and slowly spits us out
half-deafened and our blood still dyed: all this
to mask the simple dismal fact that we
decay and find our term of life is fixed.
This giant governance, a mammoth toy,
distracts us for the daytime, but the night
brings back the quiet, and the solemn dark.

God save us from ever ending, though billions have.
The world is blanketed by foregone deaths,
small beads of ego, bright with appetite,
whose pin-sized prick of light winked out,
bequeathing Earth a jagged coral shelf
unseen beneath the black unheeding waves.

*

My visitors, my kin. I fall into
the conversational mode, matching it
to each old child, as if we share a joke
(of course we do, the dizzy depths of years)
and each grandchild, politely quizzing them
on their events and prospects, all the while
suppressing, like an acid reflux, the lack
of prospect black and bilious for me.

Must I do this, uphold the social lie
that binds us all together in blind faith
that nothing ends, not youth nor age nor strength,
as in a motion picture which, once seen,
can be rebought on DVD? My tongue
says yes; within, I lamely drown.

*

I think of those I loved and saw to die:
my Grampop in his nightshirt on the floor;
my first-wife's mother, unable to take a bite
of Easter dinner, smiling with regret;
my mother in her blue knit cap, alone
on eighty acres, stuck with forty cats,
too weak to walk out to collect the mail,
waving brave good-bye from her wind-chimed porch.

And friends, both male and female, on the phone,
Their voices dry and firm, their ends in sight.
My old piano teacher joking, of her latest
diagnosis, "Curtains." I brushed them off,
these valorous, in my unseemly haste
of greedy living, and now must learn from them.

*

Endpoint, I thought, would end a chapter in
a book beyond imagining, that got reset
in crisp exotic type a future I
—a miracle!—could read. My hope was vague
but kept me going, amiable and swift.
A clergyman—those comical purveyors
of what makes sense to just the terrified—
has phoned me, and I loved him, bless his hide.

My wife of thirty years is on the phone.
I get a busy signal, and I know
she's in her grief and needs to organize
consulting friends. But me, I need her voice;
her body is the only locus where
my desolation bumps against its end.

The City Outside 12/11/08

Stirs early: ambulances pull in far
below, unloading steadily their own
emergencies, and stray pedestrians
cross nameless streets. Traffic picks up at dawn,
and lights in the skyscrapers dim.
The map of Beacon Hill becomes 3-D,
a crust of brick and granite, the State House dome
a golden bubble single as the sun.

I lived in Boston once, a year or two,
in furtive semi-bachelorhood. I parked
a Karmann Ghia in Back Bay's shady spots

but I was lighter then, and lived as if
within forever. Now I've turned so heavy
I sink through twenty floors to hit the street.

*

I had a fear of falling—airplanes
spilling their spinning contents like black beans;
the parapets at Rockefeller Center or
the Guggenheim proving too low and sucking
me down with impalpable winds of dread;
engorging atria in swank hotels,
the piano player miles below his music,
his instrument no bigger than a footprint.

I'm safe! Away with travel and abrupt
perspectives! Terra firma is my ground,
my refuge, and my certain destination.
My terrors—the flight through dazzling air, with
the blinding smash, the final black—will be
achieved from thirty inches, on a bed.

*

Strontium 90—is that a so-called
heavy element? I've been injected,
and yet the same light imbecilic stuff—
the babble on TV, newspaper fluff,
the drone of magazines, banality's
kind banter—plows ahead, admixed
with world collapse, atrocities, default,
and fraud. Get off, get off the rotten world!

The sky is turning that pellucid blue
seen in enamel behind a girlish Virgin—
the doeskin lids downcast, the smile demure.

Indigo cloud-shreds dot a band of tan;
the Hancock Tower bares a slice of night.
So whence the world's beauty? Was I deceived?

Peggy Lutz, Fred Muth 12/13/08

They've been in my fiction; both now dead,
Peggy just recently, long stricken (like
my Grandma) with Parkinson's disease.
But what a peppy knockout Peggy was!—
cheerleader, hockey star, May Queen, RN.
Pigtailed in kindergarten, she caught my mother's
eye, but she was too much girl for me.
Fred—so bright, so quietly wry—*his*

mother's eye fell on me, a "nicer" boy
than her son's pet pals. Fred's slight wild streak
was tamed by diabetes. At the end,
it took his toes and feet. Last time we met,
his walk rolled wildly, fetching my coat. With health
he might have soared. As was, he taught me smarts.

*

Dear friends of childhood, classmates, thank you,
scant hundred of you, for providing a
sufficiency of human types: beauty,
bully, hanger-on, natural,
twin, and fatso—all a writer needs,
all there in Shillington, its trolley cars
and little factories, cornfields and trees,
leaf fires, snowflakes, pumpkins, valentines.

To think of you brings tears less caustic
than those the thought of death brings. Perhaps
we meet our heaven at the start and not
the end of life. Even then were tears
and fear and struggle, but the town itself
draped in plain glory the passing days.

*

The town forgave me for existing; it
included me in Christmas carols, songfests
(though I sang poorly) at the Shillington,
the local movie house. My father stood,
in back, too restless to sit, but everybody
knew his name, and mine. In turn I knew
my Granddad in the overalled town crew.
I've written these before, these modest facts,

but their meaning has no bottom in my mind.
The fragments in their jiggled scope collide
to form more sacred windows. I had to move
to beautiful New England—its triple
deckers, whited churches, unplowed streets—
to learn how drear and deadly life can be.

Needle Biopsy 12/22/08

All praise be Valium in Jesus' name:
a CAT-scan needle biopsy sent me
up a happy cul-de-sac, a detour not
detached from consciousness but sweetly part—
I heard machines and experts murmuring about me—

a dulcet tube in which I lay secure and warm
and thought creative thoughts, intensely so,
as in my fading prime. Plans flowered, dreams.

All would be well, I felt, all manner of thing.
The needle, carefully worked, was in me, beyond pain,
aimed at an adrenal gland. I had not hoped
to find, in this bright place, so solvent a peace.
Days later, the results came casually through:
the gland, biopsied, showed metastasis.

Creeper

With what stoic delicacy does
Virginia creeper let go:
the feeblest tug brings down
a sheaf of leaves kite-high,
as if to say, *To live is good*
but not to live—to be pulled down
with scarce a ripping sound,
still flourishing, still
stretching toward the sun—
is good also, all photosynthesis
abandoned, quite quits. Next spring
the hairy rootlets left unpulled
snake out a leafy afterlife
up that same smooth-barked oak.

Fine Point 12/22/08

Why go to Sunday school, though surlily,
and not believe a bit of what was taught?
The desert shepherds in their scratchy robes
undoubtedly existed, and Israel's defeats—
the Temple in its sacredness destroyed
by Babylon and Rome. Yet Jews kept faith
and passed the prayers, the crabbed rites,
from table to table as Christians mocked.

We mocked, but took. The timbrel creed of praise
gives spirit to the daily; blood tinges lips.
The tongue reposes in papyrus pleas,
saying, *Surely*—magnificent, that "surely"—
goodness and mercy shall follow me all
the days of my life, my life, forever.

Other Poems

STOLEN

Please go on being yourself.
—from my last letter from William Maxwell, July 28, 2000

What is it like, to be a stolen painting—
to be Rembrandt's *Storm on the Sea of Galilee*
or *The Concert* by Vermeer, both burglarized,
along with *Chez Tortoni* by Manet,
and some Degases, from the Isabella Stewart
Gardner Museum, in Boston, twelve years ago?

Think of how bored they get, stacked
in the warehouse somewhere, say in Mattapan,
gazing at the back of the butcher paper
they are wrapped in, instead of at
the rapt glad faces of those who love art.

Only criminals know where they are.
The gloom of criminality enshrouds them.
Why have we been stolen? they ask themselves.
Who has benefited? Or do they hang
admired in some sheikh's sandy palace,
or the vault of a mad Manila tycoon?

In their captivity, they may dream of rescue
but cannot cry for help. Their paint
is inert and crackles, their linen friable.
They have one stratagem, the same old one:
to be themselves, on and on.

The boat tilts frozen on the storm's wild wave.
The concert has halted between two notes.
An interregnum, sufficiently extended,
becomes an absence. When wise
and kindly men die, who will restore
disappeared excellence to its throne?

FRANKIE LAINE

(1913–2007)

The Stephens' Sweet Shop, 1949.
Bald Walt at work, "butterflying" hot dogs—
splitting them lengthwise for the griddle
and serving them up in hamburger buns—
while Boo, his smiling, slightly anxious wife
(a rigid perm and excess, too-bright lipstick),
provides to teen-aged guzzlers at the counter
and in an opium den of wooden booths
their sugary poisons, milkshakes thick as tar
and Coca-Cola conjured from syrup and fizz.

A smog of smoke. The jingle at the back
of pinball being deftly played. And through
the clamorous and hormone-laden haze
your slick voice, nasal yet operatic, sliced
and soared, assuring us of finding our
desire, at our old rendezvous. Today
I read you died, at ninety-three. Your voice
was oil, and we the water it spread on,
forming a rainbow film—our futures as
we felt them, dreamily, back there and then.

DOO-WOP

Does anyone but me ever wonder
where these old doo-wop stars you see
in purple tuxedos with mauve lapels
on public-television marathons
have been between the distant time when they
recorded their hit (usually only one,
one huge one, that being the nature of doo-wop)
and now, when, bathed in limelight and applause,
the intact group re-sings it, just like then?

They have aged with dignity, these men,
usually black, their gray hairdos still conked,
their up-from-the-choir baby faces lined
with wrinkles now, their spectacles a-glimmer
upon their twinkling eyeballs as they hit
the old falsetto notes and thrum-de-hums,
like needles dropped into a groove, the groove
in which both they and we are young again,
the silent years skipped over.
                                        Who knows
what two-bit gigs and muddled post-midnights
they bided their time in? And when at last
the agitated agent's call came through—
the doo-wop generation old enough
and rich enough by now to woo again,
on worthy telethons this time around,
nostalgia generating pledges—why
was not a weathered man of the quartet
deceased or otherwise impaired? How have
they done it, come out whole the other side,
how did they do it, do it still, still doo?

HER COY LOVER SINGS OUT

> When she's in love, she says, "It totally consumes me. I want to be with that person every minute of every day. I want to sleep with him and eat with him and talk with him and breathe the air he breathes."
>
> —*from the* Boston Globe, *about Doris Day*

Doris, ever since 1945,
when I was all of thirteen and you a mere twenty-one,*
and "Sentimental Journey" came winging
out of the juke box at the sweet shop,
your voice piercing me like a silver arrow,
I knew you were sexy.

And in 1962, when you
were thirty-eight and I all of thirty
and having a first affair, while you
were co-starring with Cary Grant in *That Touch of Mink*
and enjoying, according to the *Globe*,
Doris's Red-Hot Romp with Mickey Mantle,
I wasn't surprised.

Now in 2008 (did you ever
think you'd live into such a weird year?)
when you are eighty-four and I am seventy-six,
I still know you're sexy,

---

* *Doris Day: The Untold Story of the Girl Next Door*, by David Kaufman (Virgin Books, 2008), has her born in the year 1922 [page 4], but her autobiography, *Doris Day: Her Own Story* (with A. E. Hotchner; Morrow, 1976), says she was born in 1924 [page 18]. I have chosen, in this poem, to stick with the old chronology, as something I have grown used to.

and not just in reruns or on old 45 rpms.
Your four inadequate husbands weren't the half of it.

Bob Hope called you Jut-Butt, and your breasts
(Molly Haskell reported)
were as big as Monroe's but swaddled.
Hollywood protected us from you,
the consumed you, what the *Globe* tastefully terms
the "shocking secret life of America's Sweetheart."

Still, I'm not quite ready
for you to breathe the air that I breathe.
I huff going upstairs as it is.
Give me space to get over the *idea* of you—
the thrilling silver voice,
the gigantic silver screen. Go
easy on me. *Cara*, let's take our time.

ELEGY FOR A REAL GOLFER

Payne Stewart, I remember courtesy of TV
how you nearly burst in boyish joy
when you sank that uphill fifteen-footer—
not a simple putt, and you charged it—
to win the 1999 Open at Pinehurst.

You were a butternut-smooth blond Southerner
and the plus fours made you look cocky,
and the smile with a sideways tug to it,
but you didn't deserve to die that unreal way,
snuffed out by failed oxygen in a private jet

that rode the automatic pilot up and down
like a blind man doing the breast stroke
at forty thousand feet, for hours,
with its asphyxiated cargo, till the fuel ran out
and a charred hole marred South Dakota soil.

This end, so end-of-the-twentieth-century,
would not stick in my mind as a luminous loss
had I not, while marshalling at the '99
Ryder Cup matches, on the seventh fairway
at The Country Club in Brookline, watched

the parade of golfers marching down the fourth,
pausing in foursomes to hit their second shots.
In all that parade, Payne Stewart, you
had the silkiest swing, so silky
its aftermath shimmered in air: dragonfly wings.

BASEBALL

It looks easy from a distance,
easy and lazy, even,
until you stand up to the plate
and see the fastball sailing inside,
an inch from your chin,
or circle in the outfield
straining to get a bead
on a small black dot
a city block or more high,
a dark star that could fall
on your head like a leaden meteor.

The grass, the dirt, the deadly hops
between your feet and overeager glove:
football can be learned,
and basketball finessed, but
there is no hiding from baseball
the fact that some are chosen
and some are not—those whose mitts
feel too left-handed,
who are scared at third base
of the pulled line drive,
and at first base are scared
of the shortstop's wild throw
that stretches you out like a gutted deer.

There is nowhere to hide when the ball's
spotlight swivels your way,
and the chatter around you falls still,
and the mothers on the sidelines,

your own among them, hold their breaths,
and you whiff on a terrible pitch
or in the infield achieve
something with the ball so
ridiculous you blush for years.
It's easy to do. Baseball was
invented in America, where beneath
the good cheer and sly jazz the chance
of failure is everybody's right,
beginning with baseball.

TO MY HURTING LEFT HAND

Why has arthritis, a disease of wear,
attacked you, when the right, your counterpart,
has done the work? Oh, yes—I guess in golf
you gripped the club the tighter, and at night,
to love myself to sleep, I bade you grip
my stiffened nether member while I dreamed
of copulation with an unsteadily
imagined lady, whose obliging charms
opened the path, perhaps, to drowsy calm.

By day, exerting counterforce, you held
the jar whose stubborn lid resisted all
my fingers' strength, and helped lift rocks and art books;
still, you've been the lazy brother while
the dexter one has shaken loads of hands
and lifted tons of food on fork and spoon
up to my mouth (it's true, you've done the wiping
at the other end, by some deep-seated
instinctive manual-labor delegation,
but was this work or an unmentioned pleasure?)
and written miles of lines, including these.

I grant you that, by some anomaly
of chance design, the keyboard Remington
and its word-processing successors set
beneath our hands assigned a number of
the most-stroked letters—*a*, *s*, *e*, and *w*—
to the left, and these to the lesser fingers:
many a typo has flowed forth, and a strain
felt in the digits; still, is that a cause

for breakdown now? Or can the cause be guilt—
your guilt, left hand, for being sinister?

Although you wear a golden wedding ring,
you never were uplifted in a vow
or held a torch or pulled a trigger or
pointed to a star or city on a hill.
So suffer, if you must, though part of me—
a Cain demanding, as less-favored child,
attention long withheld. In this short time
remaining to us, help me clap, and pray,
and hold fast. Pained, I still can't do without you.

CLAREMONT HOTEL,
SOUTHWEST HARBOR, MAINE

Click. Clack. Struck-wicket thud. Human ex-
clamations, mannerly. Such are the sounds
of croquet, carried by an idle breeze.
Salt water, just beyond, is steely blue,
bedecked by mooring-balls and colored buoys,
beneath a sky where tufts of cirrus hang
like combings from a pampered, moon-white dog.
Vacationland, all bays and sails and trees.

The lumbermen who rafted logs downstream,
the fishermen whose slickers gleamed through storms,
as did the struggling silver in their nets,
impart, though dead, a hardness to this coast
where, mornings, wickets on their vacant courts
make, with their shadows, rhomboidal pairs of wings.

Maine mountains, vestiges of Ap-
palachians once mightier than Rockies,
have balding tops, like men, and crumbling sides
that seek to fill the sea with scree and piles
of giant building blocks for reassembly
next aeon. Rocking on the Claremont porch
in my fortuity and gazing past
the croquet court and sail-filled, too-blue bay

and shoreline summer homes to pine-dark slopes
that hide their hiking trails, I see a spot,

below the crest, a broad gray bare spot where
I want to be, want very much, so much
a lightning crackle floods my chest with pain:
the viewer, like the view, is wearing out.

ANGEL BONES

Next to the statue-laden cathedral of Reims,
the bishop's palace has become a museum
containing many stones cast down by wear,
bombardment, renovation, and the rare
   too-thunderous Te Deum.

Huge saints and angels, retired from the weather,
stand tall above us. Their visages were carved
to show a soul—a face of grace above the wars,
the plagues, the congregational stench of masses—
   to worshippers they dwarfed.

Now chips and missing chunks give proof these hulks
on loan from Heaven fell prey to earthly harm,
for limestone, soft to sculpt, breaks easily.
Look here!—a sheared and fractured flank reveals
   a tiny shell, distinct, intact,

from vanished, darkling, long pre-Christian seas.
The pious masses, milling underneath
and looking up to holy largeness, lacked
the science to deduce from this small clue
   what mighty absence it might mean.

DEATH OF A COMPUTER

Eight years of stories, novels, book reviews—
the daily grind. *Someday it's going to crash*,
I was assured, and so, an insecure
computer dilettante, I bought a new
and tucked the old in an odd room, where, when
I plugged it in again, it took old disks
and turned them into final printed versions,
dark marks on paper safer than electrons
after all. The mechanism seemed
not to resent semi-retirement.

Today, it died; I think it died. First sign:
a ghostly square imposed itself upon
the text, like "inappropriate" behavior
that casts a shadow on a gathering but
can be ignored. Then, at the next command,
black stripes appeared, bejeweled with tiny bits
of shattered icons; it performed much as
a one-time lawyer in a senile fit
springs up to address the jury with
the trademark flourishes and folksy candor.

The pointing arrow then began to trail
black pixels like a painter's dripping brush.
Split second to split second, the monitor
believed itself to still be making sense,
while stripes and streaks and sudden twists transformed
my tapped advice into a rapid havoc;
Embarrassed by such bright and hopeful garble,
I in a spurt of mercy shut it down.
May I, too, have a stern and kindly hand
bestow upon my failing circuits peace.

COLONOSCOPY

Talk about intimacy! I'd almost rather not.
The day before, a tussle with nausea
(DRINK ME: a liter of sickly sweet liquid)
and diarrhea, so as to present oneself
pristine as a bride to the groom with his tools,
his probe and tiny TV camera
and honeyed words. He has a tan,
just back from a deserved vacation
from his accustomed nether regions.

Begowned, recumbent on one's side,
one views through uprolled eyes the screen whereon
one's big intestine snakes sedately by,
its segments marked by tidy annular
construction seams as in a prefab tunnel
slapped up by the mayor's son-in-law.
A sudden wash of sparkling liquid shines
in the inserted light, and hairpin turns
loom far ahead and soon are vaulted past
impalpably; we float, we fall, we veer
in these soft, pliant passages spelunked
by everything one eats.
                                        Then all goes dark,
as God intended it whenever He
sealed shut in Adam's abdomen
life's slimy, twisting, smelly miracle.
The bridegroom's voice, below the edge of sight
like buried treasure, announces,
"Perfect. Not a polyp. See you in
five years." Five years? The funhouse may have folded.

LEVELS OF AIR

I

spring midges near
my eyes, my ear

II

one level up, a robin rests
in a low beech bough
and dipping swallows
assemble muddy nests

III

the crows atop my oaks
let fall white shit, black croaks

IV

gulls: in from the sea,
their gray wings oaring
like ghost souls soaring
in Purgatory

V

a wide-winged hawk is pinned
to the sideways wind

VI

a Learjet (loudly) drones
as, wheels lowered, it homes
in on the local airstrip
after a (lucrative?) trip

VII

higher, a 737
banks east out of Logan

VIII

even closer to Heaven
a 747
or some such superfly
arrows out of Kennedy
to a European capital,
its silent jet trail
a snow-white rip
with a cruciform tip

IX

above it all unseen
our spaceships orbit
this floating planet
and angels preen

HALF MOON, SMALL CLOUD

Caught out in daylight, a rabbit's
transparent pallor, the moon
is paired with a cloud of equal weight:
the heavenly congruence startles.

For what is the moon, that it haunts us,
this impudent companion immigrated
from the system's less fortunate margins,
the realm of dust collected in orbs?

We grow up as children with it, a nursemaid
of a bonneted sort, round-faced and kind,
not burning too close like parents, or too far
to spare even a glance, like movie stars.

No star but in the zodiac of stars,
a stranger there, too big, it begs for love
(the man in it) and yet is diaphanous,
its thereness as mysterious as ours.

LUNAR ECLIPSE

February 20, 2008

At first, a mere tinge: the man
in the moon has turned
a shade melancholy.
His fuzzy five-o'clock shadow
deepens to a mossy arc,
a brown bite taken by hungry Earth.

Half dipped in dark, he shows
a crescent edge that we
can feebly feel as ours, our ball in space
a shadow on a lesser ball,
impervious in its momentum,
thunderous in its silence.

A bright white shard remains.
Watching the shard become a sliver,
we see our planet move:
it shoulders aside the sun
shining behind our shoulders;
it shrugs our lives away.

The disk, eclipsed, is tanned
unevenly, blotched as with blood
imperfectly dried, an ember
embedded in ashes
light years deep, its color
warm and wrong overhead.

BIRD CAUGHT IN MY DEER NETTING

The hedge must have seemed as ever,
seeds and yew berries secreted beneath,
small edible matter only a bird's eye could see,
mixed with the brown of shed needles and earth—
a safe, quiet cave such as nature affords the meek,
entered low, on foot, the feathered head
alert to what it sought, bright eyes darting
everywhere but above, where net had been laid.

Then, at some moment mercifully unwitnessed,
an attempt to rise higher, to fly,
met by an all but invisible limit, beating wings
pinioned, ground instinct denied. The panicky
thrashing and flutter, in daylight and air,
their freedom impossibly close, all about!

How many starved hours of struggle resumed
in fits of life's irritation did it take
to seal and sew shut the berry-bright eyes
and untie the tiny wild knot of a heart?
I cannot know, discovering this wad
of junco-fluff, weightless and wordless
in its corner of netting deer cannot chew through
nor gravity-defying bird bones break.

OUTLIVING ONE'S FATHER

I could feel, above me,
the hunger in his stride, the fear
that hurled him along an edge
where toothaches, low pay, discipline
problems in the classroom were shadows
of an all-dissolving chaos.

At his side, his shorter only offshoot,
I both sheltered and cowered. He was fallible
but doughty, even cocky as he drove
disintegrating pre-war cars down Reading's
rattling streets, past coal yards,
candy stores, and dives
whose lurid half-glimpsed doings amused
his Presbyterian soul, bred of a Trenton manse.

The Middle Atlantic region was the humid hell
where he showed me how to go unscorched
by neon and glaring sidewalks. He
had been there before, my guide. Now where
can I shelter, how can I hide,
how match his stride
through years he never endured?

THE OLD BILLS

How much better they were, the old bills—
Lincoln and Hamilton, Jackson and Grant,
engraved-steel faces, jabots and stocks,
high collars, wide lapels, and lips and eyes
alive and fine as those of a cornered mouse,
a killing precision in each spidery line
engraved with the fervor of a saint
going blind by the light of dying gods.

Now only Washington is still that way,
not milky and inflated and surrounded
by palely tinted anti-counterfeit
devices but plain in two greens, the gaze
unflinching in its oval, deadly and grave:
a nation-maker's unrelenting glint
insisting that this note is legal tender,
demanding we redeem it with our blood.

STRETCH

What light is tenderer
than this of early February
at 5:05 p.m. or so,
just trying brightness out?

The trash cans lie emptied
and cockeyed on the curb,
the trees in the little park
hold old snow in their shade,

but a bird's rude song pierces
the cloud of expectant twigs
while a real cloud turns magenta
in the newly prolonged blue.

TREES

Mute massive entities
that make no claims on me
beyond the odd acorn
pinging my car roof or
the heaps of autumn leaves
demanding disposal, trees
evolved life-properties
quite unlike mine—less nervous,
statelier. The bast
and cambium pass sap
from root to leaf and back,
and mute cells multiply.

Their leafy heads contain
wind motions but no brain;
their heartwood holds them firm,
unweakened by a qualm
of love, forethought, or fear.
For many million years
insensate trees played host
to borers, birds, and us.
They breathe out oxygen,
the gas that we take in,
and suck in CO_2,
which our lungs find de trop.

Benignly then, each tree
in sweetly breathing keeps
our fevered planet cool
and halfway liveable.

And yet, en masse, their aura
in darkling grove or forest
feels hostile; wordless hate
is what they emanate,
blank trunk and branching claw
protesting ax and saw,
and gracious poise destroyed
by busy-ness and noise.
Pickets within the strife
brute matter thrusts on life,
trees mother us by day,
but nightly rue our sway.

TV

As if it were a tap I turn it on,
not hot or cold but tepid infotainment,
and out it gushes, sparkling evidence
of conflict, misery, concupiscence
let loose on little leashes, in remissions
of eager advertising that envisions
on our behalf the better life contingent
upon some buy, some needful acquisition.

A sleek car takes a curve in purring rain,
a bone-white beach plays host to lotioned skin,
a diaper soothes a graying beauty's frown,
an unguent eases sedentary pain,
false teeth are brightened, beer enhances fun,
and rinsed hair hurls its tint across the screen:
these spurts of light are drunk in by my brain,
which sickens quickly, till it thirst again.

TWINKLETAPE

Woods, as we know,
can scarcely be seen:
a gray fog of twigs.
The same with cities and stars.
What glints and twinkles,
though, all the more visible
along the highways now
that it is obsolete,
replaced by CDs, is
recording tape, spilled
by the bale, by the mile
from trash trucks and
shattered tape decks,
snagged in the median strip,
festooned in roadside weeds.

How it catches the sun,
released from making music!
Magnetic tapeworms
metallic black in color
have become scintillant
dragons, invisible
save where sunbeams
crack their old code.
Dazzled and teased,
we drive along wondering
when this species of waste
will sink into earth
like the bullets of a battle,
like the fireflies
of boyhood summers.

WACO

The local Hilton, situated near
the Roeblings' old suspension bridge (a trial
attempt, it's said, for their Brooklyn masterpiece,
though built for cattle drives across the Brazos),
contains a bar where four great TV screens
befuddle breakfast eaters with a feast
of twitching imagery, the news gone mad.

Ten miles away, the Branch Davidians'
outmoded news is weathering beneath
a high gray sky; small signs stuck here and there
as on an amateurish battlefield
explain, as best they can, the school bus buried,
the compound bulldozed flat, and, still intact,
the dead messiah's battered motorcycle.

The faithful who survived (some did, and own
this land) are not in view. Instead, a yellow,
youthful mongrel cur, without a collar,
starved for affection yet with a taste for it,
whimpers, leaps, and licks our hands, abject
and wagging; the will to believe lives on
amid these miles of weeds and sorghum fields.

SAGUAROS

They look battered and friction-worn, although
they never go
anywhere, but stand for a century or two
as if playing statue
out in the humorless sun
and the cold-faced moon. Their fun
is somber fun, clumsy fun, without a word.
The hummingbird
and the cactus wren
inhabit their thorny mockery of men,
each miming gesture
slightly unprecedented in Nature.
Their melancholy individuality
spells death to me;
their skeletons outlast their flesh, as with us,
  and as in many a howling congregation
  their arms lift up in surrender or supplication.
Mute mobs of them throng the desert dusk.

Sonnets

EVENING CONCERT, SAINTE-CHAPELLE

The celebrated windows flamed with light
directly pouring north across the Seine;
we rustled into place. Then violins
vaunting Vivaldi's strident strength, then Brahms,
seemed to suck with their passionate sweetness,
bit by bit, the vigor from the red,
the blazing blue, so that the listening eye
saw suddenly the thick black lines, in shapes
of shield and cross and strut and brace, that held
the holy glowing fantasy together.
The music surged; the glow became a milk,
a whisper to the eye, a glimmer ebbed
until our beating hearts, our violins
were cased in thin but solid sheets of lead.

A WEE IRISH SUITE

Paris–Dublin, at Night

Cobwebs of orange pinpricks tinge the void
beneath our roaring wings; myriad lives
give off their sullen glow. A brighter gnat,
a helicopter beaming traffic news,
slides sideways through the thickest of the swarm;
thin filaments connect the villages
that mar the perfect earth like jellyfish
poisoning with their glow pure ocean depths.

The fertile fields of France, black lakes, give way
to Channel nothingness, an interval
too brief before the luminescences
of England spill bacillae everywhere.
The Irish Sea kills all, till Dublin's squares
of seaside lanterns shock us back to life.

Portrush, Northern Ireland

Smoking in this room, a notice says,
in the Royal Court Hotel, *can lead*
to a deep cleaning charge of £50.
The sea we see through rain-bespattered doors
that would, in summer, slide to give dead-white
new-marrieds access to a feeble sun,
supplies, like loads of eternal laundry,
onrolling breakers cresting into foam.

In restaurants with themed cuisines, the young
of Anglo-Ireland make gay with their Guinness
and a drowned backdrop of dated rock,
but bare the still disconsolate dry wit
of the colonized. These people had a war,
and peace partakes of the sea's tedium.

New Resort Hotel, Portmarnock

Too many plugs and switches in the room.
The reading lights are dim, however, and
the flat black plasma television screen
ignores the hand remote, as does the safe
the combination I distrustfully
punch in. Too many outlets for the well-
connected businessman, too much Preferred
Lifestyle, here in formerly homely Eire.

The Celtic Tiger still has crooked teeth,
the twinkle of the doomed-to-come-up-short.
Success's luxuries pair awkwardly
with golf's grim thrashing out upon the links,
the shabby, shaggy dunes where newborn rich
land helicopters, then can't find their balls.

PHNOM PENH

French touches linger in the shopworn streets—
Art Deco market like a Pantheon
in flaking mustard stucco, balconies
of lacy ironwork, and boulevards
whose breadth translates as *logique pure* beneath
the rush and buzz of fragile motorbikes
where four can ride, the smallest sound asleep,
the mother's smooth legs dangling in high heels.

Life has returned to avenues Pol Pot
once emptied with insane decrees; a school
employed as torture house has now become
a museum where the soon-to-be-dead
stare mutely from the walls. A savage dream
of order melts into a traffic jam.

MADURAI, INDIA

From our terrace at the Taj Garden Retreat
the city below belies its snarl of commerce—
men pushing postcards on the teeming street,
and doe-eyed children begging with quick words
so soft the language can't be understood
even were we to try and not to flee
the nudge of stirred pity. Can life be good,
awakening us to hunger? What point has Being?

Vishnu, sleeping, hatched the cosmic lotus
from his navel. The god-filled, polychrome,
great temple towers—glaring, mountainous—
assume from here a distant ghostly tone,
smoke shadows in the sleeping cityscape
that dreams a universe devoid of shape.

SUBCONTINENTAL

Much excrement, including elephant dung.
Food has a spicy base, and temple walls
wear sympathetic sweat four thousand years
in depth, squared by a billion prayers.
Dust dulls all things save saris and the shine
in roadside children's eyes and smiling teeth
as our ungiving bus sweeps by. Don't stop,
don't wet your toothbrush in the faucet water

of even the poshest hotel. Brought home,
an accumulated weight—Man's misery—
tugs at the bowels, and a great release
fragrant of spice, of ghee, of curry, and
of oily fingered priests, bare-chested, taints
the familiar bathroom, unreally clean.

FAIR HELEN

Helen of Troy, shining from Priam's porch,
her absent-minded gray gaze telling all
the dying, striving warriors below
that she suffices, the glorious cause
for Hector's and Achilles' men to die for,
held coiled within her a yard or two of shit,
of fecal matter waiting for its truth
to find the Turkish air and disappear.

The purplish blue of her well-hidden bowels
was not the sea-mist tint with which her gaze
accepted Menelaus and the horde
of men adoring her for giving them
the rage to die. The shit below, the shit
within are incidents; she turns and shines.

LUCIAN FREUD

(An exhibit in Venice, September 2005)

Yes, the body is a hideous thing,
the feet and genitals especially,
the human face not far behind. Blue veins
make snakes on the backs of hands, and mar
the marbled glassy massiveness of thighs.
Such clotted weight's worth seeing after centuries
(Pygmalion to Canova) of the nude
as spirit's outer form, a white flame: Psyche.

How wonderfully Saint-Gaudens's slim Diana
stands balanced on one foot, in air, moon-cool,
forever! But no, flesh drags us down,
its mottled earth the painter's avid ground,
earth innocently ugly, sound asleep,
poor nakedness, sunk angel, sack of phlegm.

ST. PETERSBURG

Acres of gold leaf, feathered into place
with squirrel tails, restored the palaces
for tourist trade. Tremendous churches, freed
from gray decades of Marxist usefulness
as barracks, atheist museums, or
warehouses for potatoes and state goods,
proclaim again the news of risen Christ
in marble, malachite, and candlelight.

Peter the Great applied to muddy marsh
alive with estuary currents stones
that paved relentless streets Italianate
in pastel tints and pillared pomp. Lean girls
in tall and pricey boots now stalk soft prey
where their grandmothers starved on hard Seige-bread.

FLYING TO FLORIDA

At Gate 16, one man is wearing sandals
though this is Boston, with a foot of snow;
toes tanned beneath their hair, he flexes them
as if in sand already. Apparel runs
to sweatpants, Nikes, nylon windbreakers.
Above our grizzled heads canned CNN
babbles half-inaudibly. For this
we braved security, smirking, afraid?

The beeping portal, the belt of x-rayed bags—
we passed their tests, to fly. What have we done
to earn eternal youth? Nothing so great—
been born American, put in our time.
Now, agèd, average, dullish, lame, and halt,
we claim our due, our fun doom in the sun.

WHITE HORIZON

Looking up from a book long immersed in,
hoping to see land beneath me at last,
I saw instead that we were over clouds
covering all trace of the Earth. My eyes
impacted upon a level white horizon,
below it sheer cloud-mass like a vast pure page,
and above it a blue so deep as to be,
almost, the fabled velvet death-black sky,
salted with stars, that only astronauts see—
astronauts, those prosaic bravos,
who bring us back mere photographs
and standard pieties from where they go,
where few have gone, like close-mouthed thieves
silvering through the dark of diagrams.

MALE VOICES, FROM BELOW

Three men repainting the kitchen under my study
never weary of talking, that plaintive baritone
of sports commentary: who should
have been traded for whom, and who
isn't worth a dime of his salary. Oh,
the monotony, not sublime, of the male—
the ceaseless thrust, the voiced aggression
toward a world of imagined malfeasance!

Couldn't the species manage without these clowns?
With an ovary-activating device,
say, installed in beauty parlors?
A trio of women would babble beneath me
like shivering leaves, like sighing wavelets;
I wouldn't understand a blessed word.

STRIPPED

Handsome young men—Brazilian, with
a mournful Greek foreman—came and scraped away
a hundred years of paint from this our home.
As a process, it was arduous,
a circumambient, besieging pecking
that also scraped the inside of my skull.
When they were done, the house loomed in bare wood,
blonder in color than expected, warm

and vulnerable, like a woman who
has lived a hundred years in bridal white
and now is naked for an interlude,
the wood her actual substance, soft, its grain
and tint so fleshly that we see at last
she loved us, these our years, enclosing us.

CHAMBERED NAUTILUS

How many rooms one occupies to lead
a life!—the child's small cell, within earshot
of his parents' smothered moans; the college room
assigned by number, a poster-clad outpost
of freedom; the married man's bedchamber,
cramped scene of glad possession and sneaking sorrow;
the holiday rental, redolent of salt
and sun and other people's cast-off days;
the capstone mansion with its curtained pomp;
the businessman's hotel, a one-night stand
whose trim twin beds and TV sketch a dream
of habitation soon forgot; the chill
guest room; the pricey white hospital space,
where now the moaning has drawn nearer still.

TOOLS

Tell me, how do the manufacturers of tools
turn a profit? I have used the same clawed hammer
for forty years. The screwdriver misted with rust
once slipped into my young hand, a new householder's.
Obliviously, tools wait to be used: the pliers,
notched mouth agape like a cartoon shark's; the wrench
with its jaws on a screw; the plane still sharp enough
to take its fragrant, curling bite; the brace and bit
still fit to chew a hole in pine like a patient thought;
the tape rule, its inches unaltered though I have shrunk;
the carpenter's angle, still absolutely right though I
have strayed; the wooden bubble level from my father's
meager horde. Their stubborn shapes pervade the cellar,
enduring with a thrift that shames our wastrel lives.

VACATION PLACE

The space grows smaller. The sense of release
has yielded to another, of an end
to possibilities in this small piece
of borrowed territory where we spend
a week or month to cease to be ourselves,
environs lighter than accustomed air,
our bureau drawers less burdened, and the shelves
of paint-free poplar innocently bare.

We heard at first all silence. Voices now,
whose owners we know, pierce the morning; cars
afflict the gravel; starlings make a row;
worn routines creak; hungry for mail, we starve.
Dear flimsy quasi-home, we'll miss your view,
but life is more than viewing; it's to do.

TUCSON

Pimería Alta—Mexico's frontier,
"high Pima land," was here ere gringo guns
and dollars came and sealed the Gadsden Purchase.
The railroad and the Rio Santa Cruz
fed an adobe strip; in civil war,
the territory turned Confederate
till Union troops from California
left only cruel Apaches in the field.

The great plain framed by four blue mountain ranges
is now a buzzing grid, where Walgreens looms
at almost every corner. Malls abound,
and winter homes—low to the sand, tan huts
of pale-faced invaders—oust cactus wrens
and cougars. The crime rate is strangely high.

THUNDERSTORM IN DORSET, VERMONT

It needs green hills to host a thunderstorm;
this grumbling giant needs a place to hide
and break his kindling into splinters,
one stick at a time, and then in bundles,
compacted threats that issue forth from where
an oily darkness reigns beyond the ridge.
The sizzle in our brains is overruled
by such triumphant voltage overload.

We witness vast concussions; something falls
down sets of stairs the bottom step of which
cracks open wide enough to show a strip,
a vein of naked light. All goes soft—
the rain unfurls in supple gusts, the leaves
flash pale, then limply steep themselves in green.

DECEMBER, OUTDOORS

Clouds like fish shedding scales are stretched
thin above Salem. The calm cold sea
accepts the sun as an equal, a match:
the horizon a truce, the air all still.
Sun, but no shadows somehow, the trees
ideally deleafed, a contemplative gray
that ushers into the woods (in summer
crammed with undergrowth) sheer space.

How fortunate it is to move about
without impediment, Nature having
no case to make, no special weather to plead,
unlike some storm-obsessed old symphonist.
The day is *piano;* I see buds so subtle
they know, though fat, that this is no time to bloom.

Light and Personal

TO A WELL-CONNECTED MOUSE

(Upon reading of the genetic closeness of mice and men)

Wee, sleekit, cow'rin, tim'rous beastie,
Braw science says that at the leastie
We share full ninety-nine percent
O' genes, where'er the odd ane went.

O nibbling, pink-tail'd, bright-ee'd sir,
We hail frae ane smal' fearful blur
'Neath dinosaur feet, lang syne—
Na mair be pestie, cousin mine.

Stay oot my larder, oot my traps
An' they'll snap softer doon, p'rhaps,
For theft and murther blither go
When a's i' th' family, bro' an' bro'.

DUET ON MARS

Said Spirit to Opportunity,
  "I'm feeling rather frail,
With too much in my memory,
  Plus barrels of e-mail."

Responded Opportunity,
  "My bounce was not so bad,
But now they send me out to see
  These dreary rocks, bedad!"

"It's cold up here, and rather red,"
  Sighed Spirit. "I feel faint."
Good Opportunity then said,
  "Crawl on, without complaint!

"This planet needs our shovels' bite
  And treadmarks in the dust
To tell if life and hematite
  Pervade its arid crust.

"There's life, by all the stars above,
  On Mars—it's you and I!"
Blithe Spirit cried, "Let's rove, my love,
  And meet before we die!"

MARS AS BRIGHT AS VENUS

O brown star burning in the east,
elliptic orbits bring you close;
as close as this no eye has seen
since sixty thousand years ago.

Men saw, but did not understand,
the sky a depthless spatter then;
goddess of love and god of war
were inklings in the gut for them.

Small dry red planet, when you loom
again, this world will be much changed:
our loves and wars, at rest, as one,
and all our atoms rearranged.

ELEGY

> Athol, Mass. — Eastern equine encephalitis killed two emus in town, state health officials said yesterday.
>
> —*Boston Globe*

Let every Eastern egg end-product grieve;
   If emus die, egrets and eagles too
Can catch an evil equine bug, and leave
   Our eager green Earth to the lark and gnu.

Each Eve in Eden finds a friendly snake.
   No bird alive outflies the final flu.
Death steals upon the duckling, duck, and drake;
   The end of Athol emus tolls for you.

COUNTRY MUSIC

February 1999

Oh Monica, you Monica
In your little black beret,
You beguiled our saintly Billy
And led that creep astray.

He'd never seen thong underpants
Or met a Valley girl;
He was used to Southern women,
Like good old Minnie Pearl.

You vamped him with your lingo,
Your notes in purple ink,
And fed him *Vox* and bagels
Until he couldn't think.

You were our Bill's Delilah
Until Acquittal Day;
You're his-tor-y now, Monica,
In your little black beret.

SWEET AS APPLE CIDER

Suicidal in Florida? Seek guidance.
Take Friday off. Go on a holiday.
Avoidance leads to trepidation,
if not dilapidation. Intimidate
and then consolidate—formidable,
yes, but also bridal, seeking solidarity
with a likely candidate, a *hidalgo*.

REQUIEM

It came to me the other day:
Were I to die, no one would say,
"Oh, what a shame! So young, so full
Of promise—depths unplumbable!"

Instead, a shrug and tearless eyes
Will greet my overdue demise;
The wide response will be, I know,
"I thought he died a while ago."

For life's a shabby subterfuge,
And death is real, and dark, and huge.
The shock of it will register
Nowhere but where it will occur.

FOUND POEM

(A Report, Complete, from the Reading, Pennsylvania,
Daily Eagle, *July 10, 1878)*

JULY 9 — Amanda Moser, while crossing
the ore fields
of Rev. T. T. Iager, tried
to walk across the mud pond,
which seemed dry. When she got
to the middle she sunk in
to her waist, but was released
after a severe struggle.

Shillington and vicinity were awakened
on the morning of the 4th
by the firing of Samuel Shilling's
cannon, and in the evening
firecrackers, rockets, Roman candles and
a small cannon were fired
at Adam Rollman's store.

Maggie Trout was swinging
under a large cherry tree
in Mrs. Schitler's orchard, when
the limb to which the swing was attached
broke, but fortunately
she escaped serious injury.

The funeral of Mrs. Miller,
of Mohnsville,

was largely attended. Interred
at Mohnsville cemetery.

Rev. H. B. Yost preached
to a large audience at Mohnsville
on Sunday morning.

Samuel Shilling's fresh cow, valued
at $50, died.

The rain here on Monday night
refreshed everything.

FOR PETER DAVISON

(On the Occasion of His Thirtieth Anniversary as Poetry Editor of The Atlantic Monthly*)*

To Peter: poet of our North Shore rocks
and salty creeks and hayey fields, the *vox*,
in short, of country pleasures filtered through
the mind of urban, literate guys like you:
a man of land. And yet an ocean claimed
three decades spent upon the bounding main—
The Atlantic! Though tons of verses crashed
against the masthead to which you were lashed
and howling winds of inspiration roared,
you kept the bilge-pumps manned, and the Muse aboard!

A Note About the Author

John Updike was born in 1932, in Shillington, Pennsylvania. He graduated from Harvard College in 1954, and spent a year in Oxford, England, at the Ruskin School of Drawing and Fine Art. From 1955 to 1957 he was a member of the staff of The New Yorker, *and after 1957 he lived in Massachusetts. He was the father of four children and the author of more than fifty books, including collections of short stories, poems, and criticism. His novels have won the Pulitzer Prize, the National Book Award, the American Book Award, and the National Book Critics Circle Award, the Rosenthal Award, the Howells Medal, and the Campion Medal. He died in January 2009.*

A Note on the Type

The text of this book was set in a digitized version of Janson, a typeface long thought to have been made by the Dutchman Anton Janson, who was a practicing type founder in Leipzig during the years 1668–1687. However, it has been conclusively demonstrated that these types are actually the work of Nicholas Kis (1650–1702), a Hungarian, who most probably learned his trade from the master Dutch type founder Dirk Voskens. The type is an excellent example of the influential and sturdy Dutch types that prevailed in England up to the time William Caslon developed his own incomparable designs from them.

Composed by Creative Graphics,
Allentown, Pennsylvania
Printed and bound by Thomson-Shore
Dexter, Michigan

FOR MARTHA, ON HER BIRTHDAY, AFTER HER CATARACT OPERATION

My blue-eyed beauty, now you see
Through plastic sharply, courtesy
Of Dr. Saintly Shingleton
And all his green-clad crew, who spun
Their miracle, ten minutes' worth,
In time to celebrate your birth
In fine detail; O Martha mine
Come count your candles: sixty-nine
—No more, no less—alight upon
A cake of love from your own
John.